THE
HAMMERED
DULCIMER

May Swenson
Poetry Award Series

THE
HAMMERED
DULCIMER

poems
by

Lisa Williams

UTAH STATE UNIVERSITY PRESS
Logan, Utah 84322-7800

Typography by WolfPack
Cover design by Barbara Yale-Read.
Cover illustration is "Salterio Tedesco" from Bonnani's *Gabinetto Armonica*.

00   99   98   3   2   1

Library of Congress Cataloging-in-Publication Data

Williams, Lisa, 1966-

The hammered dulcimer : poems / by Lisa Williams.
p. cm.

ISBN 0-87421-249-9
ISBN 0-87421-248-0 (paperback)

I. Title.
PS3573.I449754 H35 1998
811'.54—ddc21
98-9094
CIP

for
Ruth C. Talley
1915 - 1993

CONTENTS

FOREWORD

LISA WILLIAMS'S POEMS OFTEN START OUT IN SONG AND END IN EPISTEMOL-ogy, but they frequently break out into a kind of humming in the course of walking their self-generated routes. They manifest a fine ear for not only the rhythms of verse in English but for those of the argument that makes them. She can deploy, as in the poem and the lovely "A Story of Swans," a delicately modulated unrhymed anapestic trimeter (which in less skilled hands might degenerate into damped jingle), or can, as frequently elsewhere, rightly speak in tercets framed in conventional short-lined free verse and make them resonate with her own "tone of meaning," as Frost put it.

They extend a line of powerfully and actively contemplative poetry that marks some of the finest American verse of the twentieth century. One hears in so many of the poems in *The Hammered Dulcimer* an original voice modulating a major wavelength generated by Wallace Stevens, Elizabeth Bishop, and John Ashbery; one sees in them the continuing emergence of parable from sensuous presence, of meaning from things and conditions and configurations in which it had been lurking. "A Forward Spring" is perhaps central as well as typical in this matter; with an almost Marianne Moore-like resolve, its conclusion acknowledges the lesson taught by the most basic of cyclical rhythms to the moral imagination—awakening, whether of spring or consciousness—bequeaths if not what Hart Crane called "an embassy," then certainly a project:

> I saw it so clearly,
> how the spring admitted winter
> but didn't retract.
> What they call the sublime
> doesn't look away
> but looks *at*, boldly examines
> the obscure impediments
> to what it wants; sees
> itself, sees what lies ahead
> of itself, and goes forth . . .

This poet's realm is that of a guarded wonder in which questions can seem less problematic than answers, and in which the meditative process, the turning of a formulation over and over again, becomes ever more analogous to the breathing rhythms of life itself, on the one hand, and to the controlled and constructed rhythms— and there are so many different sorts of rhythm there—of poetic formulation. Wallace Stevens remarked in one of his aphorisms (which I've always wanted to see as the first line of an Emily Dickinson quatrain) "there is no wing like meaning," and I would adduce it not only with respect to that fine poem, "In the Abstract," but to the whole of *The Hammered Dulcimer* (and is that instrument something of a southern, damselled, harmonium?) as well. It is most appropriate that Lisa Williams's work receive an award in the name of that profoundly original poet May Swenson, for this is not only a more-than-promising first book but introduces an original way of looking at the world, and of looking at that very looking itself. It is a pleasure to greet it.

John Hollander

*"Sing unto him a new song;
play skillfully with a loud noise."*

THE
HAMMERED
DULCIMER

THE DIRECTION OF SHADOW

At night, the arrows of our fortune
point up and point down.
Black and inelastic,
slanted but not like sunlight,
taut as a heron's foot
or a string about to break
are the arrows of the fortune
we do not create.

The arrows of our fortune
cannot be touched, except
when a hand interrupts
their soft black filaments
on the ground, and the skin's
color, brushed with absence,
suddenly dims—

Magnificent
are the arrows of our fortune
when the shadows of huge trees,
slender, pillared, excellent,
form them. Like the doorway
of a new religion
they open something
but what?

To the arrows of our fortune
something sometimes happens:
the force of the arrow
slings past its shadow
which drops
on the grass, on the ground,
heavy as a man.

What is left behind,
what flaps in the wind,
is not it at all—
not the vibrant quiver,

nor the impenetrable mark,
nor the piercing matter.

The man falls on the grass.
His shadow joins him.
The goal dissolves in space.
A force flies through the universe,
winged in flame.
It is a game
where nothing wins
and everything of course is lost.

SUNDAY MORNING

So this is beginning:
day entering the long field
voiced and plumed,

noise entering the mind's
accruement of dream.
It is always a struggle,

the constant waking
from inward pattern
to outward motion,

from sleep to distraction
and back again.
While around us, the sounds

of so much affluence,
details prickling the air,
a sensory cacophony

of things and more things
lifted out of despair,
the black rush of distance.

What does it matter
how true they are?
These are what we wait for,

this multiplicity
of throats and feathers,
a busy consciousness

landing on the rigid bushes
and windblown grasses,
cattails nodding in assent

as if they understood
the physical completely.
I sit on a porch

looking out at the morning
and it feels like a precipice
between the known and the unknown.

It seems a miracle
that we are not always afraid,
our many thoughts crowding

the singular present,
an untidy flock
without tangible wings

in a tangible mist,
sweeping in from the cold
to shriek of vividness.

The mind would carry the world off
but where would it land?
The real is landlord here,

you can smell it in the wind
although, if the dew is to be believed,
this field is primed

and open, it is vulnerable
to the claws of possibility,
to the multicolored being

intertwined with rays of sun.
It will come over the mountain,
flying, flying,

while the two halves of the self—
one the resting body,
the other the mind unable

to lie on the ground—
stay on their precipice,
inextricable twins

that do not understand
what they have come to find
but willing to wait for something

partly sublime.

INTERRUPTION OF FLIGHT

The woman with no feet sits on the porch.
Before her, on the new-mown lawn,
her son polishes his motorcycle
until its chrome facets gleam
under the sun, display a world
playing on surfaces, things shining along
and across, their parameters warped,
motions churning and strange. The tall trees
fringe space, fringe the blue
with its frills of white mist,
its patched lace. The old woman
watches over the humming engine
while her son revs it up,
dark roar in our ears full of wind.
The space around shapes
is of interest, the space between leaves
imprecise, planes of pale air notched
by the green, a geometry raised,
what might be an angle
interrupted by branches grown past
plain. The woman's legs jut out:
one longer, cut off below the knee,
the other lost mid-thigh. And above,
the air writhes with birds, the sky's alive
with flying into, flying through.
Robins, dark robins, and sparrows,
like strong priests, loop together
the light between edges,
gathering sense, making of the jaggedness
something defined only by feeling.
Or the crowd of the self's lifting off,
carrying an image it believes
is immense. Now the woman
with feet made of air, with no speech,
is being helped out of a car.

(When did she disappear?)
"Lean forward. *Lean forward*," the son orders.
(I was watching the birds.)
"Push yourself out! Push yourself out!"
And the world above words, the real sky
trailed by robins, by two crows
and by fat pigeons scuttling
the attic, feathering the heart's box.
One particular tree across the street
from the woman with no feet
stands in front of me. In the tree's
knotted limb is a hole, and in that waits
an additional hunger
deepening. Sparrows dart
in and out of the hole in the limb
where the restless chicks wait
with black throats. The parents
are solicitous, swooping down
every few minutes. They will not stop
so much emptiness, or the young naked song,
song so sure of the spirit's
primacy, of the terrible wish.
"Good job. That makes it easier on everyone."
Now the brusque son has placed his mother
in a wheelchair, pushed her back to the porch
where she'll sit and observe
the sun's anger increase,
the mechanical fruit. And her feet made of air
have flown off with my heart
like the birds who are priests.
May we scatter in peace.

YELLOW BIRD

Where, oh where, has my yellow bird gone?
Has he gone to the ocean? Has he gone to the town?

He has stitched up the steeple with hardly a sound
and the bells haven't rung, haven't rung.

Where, oh where, has my yellow bird gone?
Does he sing in the orchard? Does he sleep by the pond?

He has plucked a black spider and swallowed it down
and he leaves its torn web on the ground.

Where, oh where, has my yellow bird gone?
Have his feathers been scattered, like leaves in the wind?

He has flown to the well where his shadow falls in
as he lands on the stones of its rim.

Where, oh where, has my little life gone?
Have I nothing to guide me, and cold days to come?

I have seen his bright body approaching the sun
and his feathers have turned into flame.

WHAT THE WIND SAID
TO THE GIRL WHO WAS AFRAID

When he comes for you, that dark gentleman, fear,
tell him you already know him,
that you're not the foolish bride that he thinks,

that even in the crevices and chinks
of your own mind, things get carried away.
That you gaze into the arms

of trees, into a vacant night
where desire tears every dream apart.
That you walk on a path and hope it will stray.

That each twist from what's safe breaks a wish
like a curious seed
where the weeds of the wilderness mesh.

He can have the run of your house.
He can have the ruin of your grace.
He and the sadness that keeps circling nearer,

like a song you were born with and slowly remember,
like a song you were humming, and later divine.
That fine-limbed and bold as the delicate deer

on the gold hill at morning, whose legs turn to stone
at a sound, but who doesn't stop chewing the leaf
on its tongue while its body stands frozen, aware,

you believe in the constant infringement of pleasure.
You believe in the hill of your pleasure, not fear.
You too will not run. Your life will be moving

its teeth when he comes. He'll be bitten in half
while the wind in your spirit whips over the grass.
Oh how pure is that wind! It runs harder and faster

than death. It runs like a silvery fox,
like a flourish of foxes who don't have a doubt.
And you will push fear, that dark gentleman, out.

THE FALL

For Milton's Satan
heaven was a chill place,
too much already realized.

He had nothing to taste.
What he hadn't yet seen
seemed to him like real paradise.

Sometimes, beauty means
an ecstatic indifference
that freezes the heart.

It is cold. It is cold.
And it stays on its throne.
But you have to begin,

as a woman begins
when she turns from observing
the face of her youth

in a glass or a mirror—
the face she had once.
It's that turn to existence

when you stop thinking *Am I?*
or *Should I?* or *When?*
but instead, *I'm outside*

the cold dreaming of heaven.
I have fallen at last,
and you enter the world.

THE TENDERNESS
for Neil

A strong doe running with her young
is an unfathomable thing. In this late light
the trees form a craggy embrace

for her searching, and nothing's at rest.
Not the hill, not the fawn she defends,
not the pasture of clover and grass

but pursuance of movement itself
is her meaning—the absence of stone.
From embankment to thicket to lawn

that running must be her existence.
Sometimes she is splintered. Sometimes
her own child and its tenderness catches

on the adamant surface of flight—
We are lucky to come upon this
as we barrel headlong through the world

in our hard, narrow armor of self,
to come upon some kind of tenderness
turned, for a moment, to us.

Even if we stand defenseless
and certain to lose what we want,
we are lucky to notice her stop

in the grey morning mist, the sharp upward
incline to the heart of our forest,
this fleeting but palpable guest.

THE HAMMERED DULCIMER

The novice can't use her hands well.
Their frailty reminds her of twigs
but she tries to make sounds. First she holds,

very lightly, between timid fingers,
the foreign, cool weight of a hammer
(so small) made of maple or spruce

and nervously taps several strings.
Her next notes aren't crystalline bells
but splintered, exploding, with trouble,

the questions discordance inspires.
Is this me? Will the painful get better?
The girl sits alone in a room,

or else she's surrounded by faces.
No matter. She's lost in the order
her flapping hands make: tiny errors

eked out of her into the air
that crash on her body like water.
But the fine strings lie under each hammer.

Over those, her bent body casts shadow,
a flat but imperious shadow
more sprawling, more dark, than the dulcimer's

wood. Oh the intimate shadow!
A raven hunched down in late sun
in her yard closes wings not in prayer

but downward, to heed small dark thoughts.
This raven, which seems nihilistic,
shifts and flickers: green, indigo, violet,

as if some new garden were opened
in darkness to please the great sun
who sits on her throne of blue weather.

More slowly, an insect discovers
rough orange wings, bright green feet, whatever
its form needs to burst into song.

And the raven believes it is best.
And the insect has found its own rhythm,
a low parchment hum, as the dulcimer

responds to her troublesome fingers
(or responds to the small wooden hammers,
for through those, she must reach the fine strings).

The girl's back stays turned on the shadow
which hulks in the wings of her music
while the people in mind or around her,

growing bored now, begin to complain:
"This novice's noises make trouble.
We want more than all her harsh fumbling.

We want her to play a *real* song."
But she finds this new failure exciting,
as if minor spaces broke open

in the sounds she thought major, complete.
So she tries to ignore the pale sounds
of the people who murmur in protest;

it's essential her effort be focused
not on song, but on what guides her heart
through resemblances plucked on the strings . . .

The flat shadow waits. It expects
her to straighten. She's turned to the dulcimer
though the people are drifting away,

drifting far from the fields discord brings,
and the raven, the intricate insect,
are nestled in burgeoning trees.

"We know what we like," think the people.
You're playing it wrong, cries the dulcimer.
A chord hovers over the strain.

COMPLAINT

There is no mother in this night,
only the trees, with their strong backs,
their proud chests curved over the creek.

There is no mother. Why did we think
if we walked into darkness we would find her?
Why did I think

if I asked you for nothing, you would find me?
Walking into darkness is like
walking into an absence of questions:

there's a kind of peace settling down,
an inestimable reference,
a lack of desperation.

The wind goes on its way.
The eyes move through the grass.
Description takes its place

piece by piece, loss by loss.
There is no mother in this night
which pours its warm limbs over us

like a lover without motive,
without hidden interests,
like a lover that simply is.

It is good, how the self exists
and would be centered, strong, and proud
in its own right.

EVE, AFTER EATING

It had nothing to do with God,
what had made her
plunge her teeth into fate,
and nothing to do with hunger.
The shape of her lust
was not one of those globed fruits.
Nor was the pleasure
of pulp on her tongue
as simple as Truth
spilling seeds in the mind.
The snake wasn't so clever,
"Empress" this, *"Goddess"* that.
She saw through his compliments.
It was simply a choice,
to open an error,
to pluck from the branch
of knowledge and abundance
as it had been defined.
Her mouth filled with juice.
Her blood filled with song.
The plant at the center,
the growth in the heart,
the self and its lover,
are joined in this art . . .
A strange afternoon.
Afterwards,
she lay on the ground
listening to the wind
as it paused in the orchards,
hoping they wouldn't come yet
—death, god, the man.
She needed to think for a while,
and to learn.

MAN WALKING

In the evening when walking
he looks on the scene
with an eye full of time.

See, say the trees standing tall.
Us, say the clouds floating high.
Aim, say the stalks in a row.

And he wants to drift up
where the first twigs erupt
in the bright, in the cold,

where their cracklings delineate
finer and finer
small strokes of intent—

like an orderly art.
In the evening when walking
he looks on the scene

with its blue simple light
and would like to be bold.
Here, says the burgeoning mud.

You, say the houses of wood.
Move, says the moon to its kind
through the branches that cover the mind

and it goes when he goes,
and it stops when he stops,
like a rhyme.

BLACK HORSES

Black horses on a yellow hill
against a clouded sky.
How can desire go unfulfilled

or run from you and I—
Not run, but simply wander past
as if it had the wish

to find a greener circumstance
beyond our small request.
Black horses on a yellow hill

so stalwart, so serene.
What the heart may want today
does not a lifetime mean.

Longing, like those bodies dark
and curved with skin and bone,
may find a hill, may find a dale,

but not a solid home.
Black horses on a yellow hill
against a clouded sky.

Not any creature, good or ill,
can calculate the eye.

THE GROWTH

I heard a weed cry in a dream
let me in, let me in.
It grew on a hill outside my window,

was gnawed by cicadas, taunted by crows,
but still had five leaves
large as tortoises, and near the earth

a stem rotted brown. How the roots thrived
I couldn't guess, but in my dream
the weed bent its stem and slid

down to the luminescent pane
next to my bed, where I lay thinking
about pain. I saw its fringed head

nod. I saw the liquid drum
through its huge green vein.
It looked and looked at my infant life

until I felt my heart crack,
disintegrate, and swell up in my throat
like a brilliant adventure

that hadn't yet occurred.
And I woke up and whispered
(for the dark seemed fruitless)

Oh rancid, blooming mystery,
how long before your messenger
will come for me?

MANNERS, 1977

My grandmother took me for a ride
in her brand new turquoise glide
of a car, with doors for fins.

We sank in the fabulous plush,
soft leather like family skin,
the windows opening at will.

Wish had become mechanical.
My grandmother steered the way
through complicated streets,

through the old, Southern sights.
We moved in clouds of blue:
hot blue, Amazon River blue.

We were partners in luxury.
The sidewalks jumped, then disappeared.
Birds sprang in various directions.

We were calm. We didn't care.
There were tiny, tree-lined roads,
and streets of rowdy schoolchildren.

We passed the hospital, the pharmacy,
the house behind the highest fence,
another house we'd lived in once,

its same old willow weeping.
My grandmother had silver hair
that dazzled anyone who noticed.

She'd worked for years at duty.
The Lincoln suited her slow beauty.
We passed, serenely,

our favorite, blooming neighborhoods,
vast mansions we would never enter
—that is, would never see together.

The sun was certain; the sky one view.
No news of what lay just ahead.
Or was it miles and miles of pleasure

as we stretched our azure limbs?
Only my dazzling grandmother
could make the whole town take us in.

She taught me then (and many
years of colors later)
what distinctive manners meant.

A SPIDER

So many lines about the wind I weave.
So many lines, some of them taut

with particular gestures, some of them caught
on the edge of a house, or torn

and flapping in a violent storm.
So many thought-weighted, rock-ripped, time-worn

in the obstacled present.
No two the same, none spun as magnificently

as I aim them to be, most blown away.
All I can do is wind what courses through

my spirit, trembling instrument—old battered frame
on which the elements pour, play on, accrue

(I'd call it a lyre, but that would be too gay)
then send those filaments of soul

into sheer absence, needling the material
with a pronged and strange capacity.

The lines I make begin to shake things free
and yet fold brilliant glimmers of their colors

into a tapestry both false and brave.
At first, I only grasped the threads of others

but soon learned all would break, and none would save.
So many lines about the wind I weave.

THE MAN BY THE RIVER

The man by the river let no one in.
The man by the river grew pale and thin.
He lived in a house on the edge of the woods
where the marsh wind blows and the dark creeps in.

On days of sun he'd stay inside
and pace, and question himself out loud
why his true love left, why his mother died,
why a vulture circled the wide blue sky.

On days the air turned damp and dim
he'd walk from his house and the wind-tossed pines
down his father's hill to the changing strand
where waves of green met grains of sand.

The wind plucked on an instrument
that no one human hand could fit.
He watched the restless sea and land
find lines of truth to move beyond.

He watched the waves sweep twigs and bones
to shore, and sweep them back again
more fragile from the dry, hot sun.
The wind rolled dreams along the sand.

The light passed over his youth one day.
And flocks of dark birds lighted down
each year for the seeds on his father's land
and the berries that clung to his father's tree.

BANQUET

The daffodils are expectant.
On the fringes of Spring
they are waiting.
Be glad. Spread cheer.
Do not let the fabric
of joy disappear.
Benevolence
must be like this, appearing
suddenly on the margins
of our lust for change.
It is close. Too close.
We grow used to it
with its colors and bells,
its bright, slippered feet.
Delight, delight,
the soul is right,
say the daffodils. Tonight
may be their last. The meadows
confused with praise
—warm mild days—
then the crotchety winter
laying his rough hands
on the flower beds.
What is it he wants with them?
Their hopes are not hidden.
They open themselves
completely,
as if they want to be touched,
gold empty cups
for someone to fill.
They are not so innocent.
They would feel and feel.
The liquor they offer
is consciousness.
Even if he drains them,

even if he destroys
their silks and stems,
he will have to go home
eventually, he will have to retreat
from the garden alone.
Of this, they're aware.

TO NIGHT

I don't want to be afraid of you
and yet I am.
You are the tapestry
of my mortality.
You are the arbor of sound
when sound is through with me,
threats and grasses plaited through your hem.
And in the deeper places,
the center I can't thumb,
there are colors, chants,
descriptionless
wild faces.

If you are a woman
you have burdens.
You were never light.
Socrates felt that night
was when we start to see,
when the philosophers
emptied their hands
of common pleasure:
no figs on plates,
or wine,
or wordless measure,

just perfect quiet
as the soul sinks
and wisdom rises
from the lower kingdom
where she holds court
with her noble spirits . . .
She would not abandon
the light of the mind
that had shown
such graces—
and Socrates was about to die
when he explained this.

ON THE NATURE OF BEAUTY

There are so many edges to things:
this lamp, this wall, this table.
Tonight, even a question
has clean dimensions. Outside, sounds rise
through aisles of grass,
ridges of bark, larva, wings.
There are so many edges to things;
for instance, the tablet of dusk
has been broken into pieces
by darkening trees
or whittled, maybe, by an old artiste
sitting on his porch in the sky.
Who is in love with wholes,
with the blurred manteau
of evening, eternally floating down
over every brittle figure,
turning them into the ground?
Who wouldn't rather create a figure,
regal, discontinuous,
surreal and extraneous,
but as essential to the sky
as the eye is?
On land, there are so many edges,
we have to hold on to them
dearly, they become our anthem,
what we run our tongues over,
what we run our hands over,
the bodies we touch,
the lines we engage,
even the loves we leave behind
to move onto the hard, lonely stage
we are always on the verge of.
We do not really want to be saved
from the shortcomings
of hands. We do not want the whole,
serene, mellifluous, unscaled,

though we may strive to get a look at it.
So when we find the beautiful,
whatever it may mean,
however it is changing,
we feel the presence of something
(maybe it *is* wings)
sprouting, prickling, burning,
giving us the edges again
of our own limited range,
spurring the fenced-in being
—when we lay eyes on it,
the beautiful,
the thing that stops our heart,
the act that seems worth a good try,
and it is, even for a minute,
that being ready to fly.

ROMANTIC RELIEF

The trees look like women in beautiful dresses,
the blue sky their background of cloudy excesses.
To be all alone in a difficult world

is not what we're fearing. They dangle their tresses
as if they were women with answers, not guesses.
To be all alone in the world isn't hard.

These plunges of feeling, these lithe, stubborn branches
of brown and bright green, these decorative phrases
that seem like a frivolous dance in the mind . . .

We know how to be with ourselves in the world
say the women. They move to an army of breezes.
Who cares if there's not a whole army of words,

strong soldiers, to take the slim trees in their arms
and lavish their bodies with verbal caresses
until they are calm? Who cares if a world

where the soldiers, the women, the phrases are held,
isn't real? *We stay with ourselves and are charmed.*
The trees are grown women and innocent guesses

and words in the air and abstractions and bards
of some deeply historical verse in the heart.
The women are laughing. The branches grow firm,

the green leaves transgressive. *We all fall apart.*

NEGATION

The self does not find itself in the long road.
The self does not find itself in the dimming sky.
The self does not find itself in the couple with the baby
who smile as if they know where, when, and why,

nor in the mountains rising heavily
like the bent backs of monks, indifferent and old,
nor in the ruddy vegetable garden
where a figure works quietly, at the center of the world.

What it is not seems to have no end.
A river of silence is all it contains,
winding and winding through mysterious forests.
Maybe it is better not to see what is missed,

to just float on the surface of billowing dusk
where distinguishing edges are melting like lovers
and the air turns a dense and improbable hue
softening, for a minute, the absence of an 'I' and a 'You.'

LANDSCAPE

In the neighborhood of sorrow
we move because we grieve.
The houses are low and squat,

the air heavy, the boughs gnarled
with bending toward light.
If you walk along that winding street

shadowed by fate
you might hear music
drifting out of a window, someone playing

not quite well, not quite badly,
a tune that means nothing to you.
In the neighborhood of sorrow

things go about their business:
the birds, bees, etcetera,
almost indivisible

from the monotone sky
except for a small cry
here and there, the casual humming

of eternity. In the underbrush
you'll still find the twining, lush
insistence of a life—

these vines, for example,
coiled around what's young
and delicate: birch, ash, Virginia pine—

but that's just denial
doing what it can.
At one house, a cat

lays a truth from the forest
on the doorstep—a dead infant snake,
raw stomach, smooth new back

of yellow gems. The practiced griever
opens the door
to find it, then throws it in the garden,

its 's' shape of despair
landing lightly on the weeds
and sprung impatiens. Knowledge

spreads into the background
and day begins.
Across great distance, the whine

of a saw, someone taking care
of chaos. Elsewhere,
someone isn't.

A WIND IN PLACE
after Stevens

The day is green and blown
but her mother was strong
as these trees bending in the wind.

The clouds are full of avowals
but her father had the clarity
of rain-scrubbed altitudes.

There is nothing whim can't change
but the buried, nothing it can't sway
but the ground.

Now their thoughts are thinnest air
above the tangle of intelligence.
Now their touch drifts

blurred and down.
The wall between the self and wind
is just a limited perception, the eye's redress.

In the wide light,
in the blaring continuity of it,
over the dark and scrambled green,

white blooms like sudden freedoms
lift the harsh bark
as possibility raises the eye up

from its body, distinguishes its backdrop
from ordinary scenes
and from the leaves, those same spun leaves

that weigh the branches down.
But in between the wind and eye
is the interrupting wall

and the figure in place behind it
who sees the lashed events
and feels unsafe.

CRATER

Old moon, old moon,
what do I tell you?
You sit there, scribed with night.

Do you expect invention?
Beauty as its own reign
or arrangement? No praise

then, just this stutter
between stare and star, the imprint
of my heel on relative dark.

Fool moon, fool moon,
what do you know
of me or my crumbled ladders?

You're not a smile, or a grimace,
you're not even a leap,
just some bruiting glow

that hangs from its one
dichotomy. You can't figure
the tunes, the variant

weights on a tongue.
Poor moon, poor moon,
what does your one eye mean?

To have half a sense,
a cruel bright, your whole vision
wandering, or dispersed

into clueless trinkets
you can never collect.
Won't you always be

swivelling? Bold mood, your flood
is the flood of the mind
in its black habit:

lighting all, but uplifted by none.
Lantern of the odd soul,
miner of discontent,

don't come out, don't come out.
Stay hidden, in my cold coat
pocket.

ON A WORM DESCENDING A THREAD

This gray light is full of invention,
of the rustling of feathers and hues.
There are voices no language can sing.

The sun dips its face in the dark,
in the alternate substance, the mirror.
It is listening. It listens to water

and it follows that sound to the sea
where the moon waits, the delicate daughter,
earth's eldest, who sprang out of grief

and flew off through the torn, broken trees,
past the ferns, past the sisterly branches,
past the swan's neck, the forest of eyes

and of wounds, and adjusted her grace
to a height, to a distance, where sorrow
can turn from its body, not touch.

Her departure has scattered a shell
in the sea, has inflected the deep
murk of absence with silvery scales

that will brush an oiled brethren all night.
We are light, we are light, dream the fish
as the water rings out and away.

Since the darkness will flood into me,
I will rise and give birth to myself.
Oh what veils I'll remove as I go!

thinks the moon. She has thrown off her grief
and is able to shine on most nights,
then returns to a river of doubt.

Those below her must travel with care.
They must follow their stream to the end.
They must follow the stream of their listening . . .

and the grey light is full of invention,
and the soul rides the question, its string
in the musical night. The soul rides

on a frail and invisible thread
or a sound. *How it twists in the air!*
laughs the moon, looking pale, looking wan.

A STORY OF SWANS

The young girl's description of swans
is the story of swans that begins,
"As the cool lilies cover the water,

as a mellow sun gilds the wet banks,
the young man and the woman hold hands . . ."
Not the story that, glistening, rises

with algae and mud on her skin,
that is scratched by rough sedges and weeds.
Not the story where mirrors come in,

where a lack of them, in the pond's surface,
keeps wisdom from seeing her face.
Now the serpent, the subtilist creature,

lurks deep in the body of hosts.
I could tell her about the white raven
turned black for its criminal tongue,

for its shrewd and dividing intelligence
and the depth of its throat, like wild space.
How its feathers were too dim to last

in the air of such space. But her swan
is eternal, with calm, dipping suns
and a castle beyond. The rare swan!

When it floats, it floats holding its wings
firmly down. And the fermented gold
of the sun pours a mead on its skin,

on its feathers, those odd, ancient flutes
that will ferry grief out and away
through the qualms of each figure, the myths

of each word that encircles the pond.
Will you enter? The pond is obscure.
There is something about empty space,

the mistake of a hollow that charms her,
that tempts her. She peers into holes,
any hole; a cement crack, a drainpipe.

I watch her. She bends lower. Squats
to consider the back of that throat.
When you lie on your back in the dark

you will hear it come breathing, come breathing,
the fear, not the one you adore.
When your doubts rose, it rose. It had seen

you grow soft, like a powerless swan.
I could tell her about the young prince,
the bold son of the sun king, who begged

to take off in his father's fierce coach
wanting fire of his own. How the horses
who carried the light were confused

and flew higher and higher, afraid.
He fell terribly free of the coach.
He fell flaming and far into water,

and his cousin, who hated the fire
and the heat that devoured his young friend,
spent his long days lamenting near green

and cool waters, near flexible reeds
and sad willows, near bank-blossomed fruits,
searching, searching the ground for a mist

to dissolve in, until he was bent
and just lifting his feet. So the swan
that would always love water, loathe heat,

grew from this—from this grieving alone.
I could tell her the story is clear:
That the swan is a flowering grief.

That the swan is a terrible clamor.
Sorrow's face. Or the infinite stretch
of the infinite loss of first pleasure.

One who knows underneath it is hollow.
One whose wings cover serpents and hosts.
Will you float? Will you circle the pond?

Will you enter the story yourself?
I could tell her beneath the dull waters
where fins, purling muscles, quick gleams

flash the dark, there's the body of dreams.
To be wise is to know many sorrows,
is to know many holes where you stand,

to unearth the dark cry under feathers.
To be wise is to know many fires
pouring over the flesh, the small soul

on its quest. How the quest burns the whole.
And the sun, the high sun, lets it happen,
lets us rise in the rose-colored dawn . . .

but she flies from my shallow reflection.

GOD PUT THE NOOSE AROUND
MY NECK

I stood trembling and shy
on a chair of this world,
stood there, poised in between

my own life and loose space.
"Love" the bent shadow of him
adjusting, adjusting,

with purposeful hands
the contraption of threat.
"Love" the tying of knots,

fingers oiled in their skill,
the sharp hinges of elbows
framing dark work,

the tense forearms like hills,
and his breath in the distance,
that sole, vivid warmth.

God the sad, God the ghost,
all bravado and edges
in the place between things.

I could tell he was nervous
when he touched my life tenderly
under the rope,

when he kissed my soft throat
after looping his threat.
While I carefully stood

on a chair of this world
a hair's breadth from loose space.
You'd think God wouldn't do this,

that I'm somehow disgraced
by such wicked imbalance,
by the rope white as bones

snaking close to my face.
But I saw through his act.
I saw God's human face.

It was bound up in mine
and it needed my willingness.
How far would I go

to uncover my faith,
to discover my life,
the sheer weight of the self?

It was good not to fall.
And he tightened my throat
with the length of his fear,

to the shape of his want,
and he pulled at my soul,
tugged it this way and that—

But he couldn't reach through
the tight web of our difference.
He knew this, and wept.

THE GRASSHOPPER

It is a cunning thing:
woven, it would appear, of grass blades
and large as a hand, its hymn

some vast, internal drum.
Antennae waving at the newest sound
it bristles when I approach

as if the wall inside my house
were all in the world
to lean on. I imagine

a soul is like this: driven
to feel narrowed, more acute
in a chosen exterior,

some grumbling carapace.
It waits, pristine as glass,
a wordless, hardened angel

with marble, all-seeing eyes.
How do I catch the spirit
then set it free intact?

Now my jar snags
a recalcitrant leg, the insect foams,
flails curious dimensions,

and, when "freed," limps off
grotesque and frivolous
against the grass. Maybe

some liberation lies
in being out of place, out of a home,
movement itself should be a home

where error has a space . . .
but I'll fixate on the gleam.
Am I its host?

Or does it, green and surly,
unhinge the luminescent world,
this papery self that leaps and leaps

until a broken leg or wing
(mauled by the usual downfall)
looses it from the body

and it can really spring.

THE END OF SPRING

There is betrayal in such sudden change.
We do not own it, this froth
of heat drowning our efforts,

making us frown at the day's complete,
exhausting utterance. Minute
after rayed minute rains down,

on the sidewalks, in the corners of rooms,
in our throats, and we are too tired
to take the change apart. We give it a name.

Summer, we say. *The end of spring.*
Flowers like lost grips,
dried and slouched with disappointment.

Birth crawled into a crevice.
Wasps flying through window cracks, withered, enraged.
Last week, something raised its head

and wild winds rolled
from the Blue Ridge to the pine-covered hill
behind my house

downing three pines over it. The broken trees
we chopped and hauled away,
polishing off the initial mess

with carefulness. Every season
shreds the deeply appreciated
flares of the last.

Destruction. Creation.
There is no good way to distinguish
between the two. And our art isn't much different.

We like to pretend
it stands clear, but it's always in flux.
It moves. It falls.

It is. The weather of the world,
the weather of the mind. It finds us.
The way two goldfinches,

the male with his black angled hood,
the female brownish and earthly,
return to my garden every afternoon.

The way their species,
elusive, yet too well-known,
threaten to flicker my every poem

with the usual cliché,
though I have yet to catch their sublimity.
I promise myself

I won't let them in, but what can I do?
I can't fight the refrain,
what returns to the setting,

returns to the poem,
and does not grow tired of the vast, enduring
background. I'd guess

that is poetry:
not flight, but things coming back
where they're wanted, comfortable

—haunts
of detail—while the rest, the god or goddess,
the uniform reign,

lingers behind, never known
in its entirety,
heavy and gray, burnished and green,

a tapestry so prevalent
we hardly see it,
the monstrous "yes" that does not change

slipping over the hills into our hands,
our feet, our eyes flooded with what
could be peace

in the star-flecked night.

IN THE ABSTRACT

Slowly, slowly, slowly,
a red hawk circles the blue sky.
"It is a meaning,"

I could say, or "It is matter,
the *form*." But that would be
disingenuous.

How a word
soars from us, leaving
the mind open, the mouth empty.

Or, alternately, how it stabs at
the small distinctions
on land, conquering

deep untidiness
shallowly. So my guess,
placid and many-hued,

doubles the blue
distance, which is almost all
slate.

So it falls.
If meaning were flight,
would it be so perfectly honed,

would it be such an instrument
of departure,
such a private chariot

of feather and air?
And what would that meaning
find, the one

we can't touch, clear and sure
of its path?
How it would swath

through the blue shell
of absence, not even a cry
could reach, not even a cry

on the highest of hills . . .
Oh well. If I
am not careful, the meaning's

lost. Maybe
it is what appears to be
most vulnerable

to loss: a word
and its history, its freight,
the wing that lifts

our eyes to see beyond sight.

AMBIVALENCE

It is hard to believe
as alive as we are
that on certain afternoons

—say this one, with its gray streams of light
into corners of rooms
and its mild open air

and its orthodox cries
from lowest heaven—the soul can wander
to and fro

without knowing what to do,
can be heavy with longing
without longing for,

and the feet can carry the body
across floor after floor
without going anywhere

beyond their own plain action.
Then there is no satisfaction.
Then yearning, in fact,

may be all we can find.
At such times, the heart wants—
To draw back? To lie still?

We can't tell.
The flesh holds out its hands,
two lumps of desire,

silver in the fallen light,
tarnished with rifts, portents, years . . .
They can bear no answer.

THE CHANT

Why can't I sing myself awake
when darkness falls, when darkness falls,
or bring myself to brightly make

a difference to my dragging soul
since differences, as we've been told,
are those that we ourselves create?

The crickets know a constant beat
in pointed grass and shadowed hill
as silence threatens to repeat,

when darkness falls and fear unfolds.
There they are, hunched and chanting still,
an independent opposite

to all the rings of quiet black.
But I can't simply rise and break
this ring of silence in my heart

or lift a hand to interrupt
the evening that is closing down.
I stay behind, I hesitate,

as leaden as a lying bell.
The sky is like an empty shell
and inside that, small instruments,

beyond all expectation, leap,
as darkness falls, as darkness falls.
Their sound is sharp. They reconnect

the quiet land to distant stars
and lift, in tiny increments,
some figure out of deepest thought.

When both our bodies wandered here
and never thought to hesitate
but did and meant, since they were near

those differences two souls can make,
then evening held, and fear was old,
and morning had a human shape.

A FORWARD SPRING

Today the cold came back—
a sudden estrangement.
That first pale decision
to reach as far as lushness can
had just broken through:
all the celebratory leaves
explored by squirrels,
the return of canopies
instead of high naked trees,
deer in new horns
stepping over the folded
carnage of winter storms,
worms winding
like thought through those layers
where only a future had roots
during periods of doubt,
the mysterious wet dirt,
and the sun's intelligence
that separates clouds
with rays of sheer will.
I saw it so clearly,
how the spring admitted winter
but didn't retract.
What they call the sublime
doesn't look away
but looks *at*, boldly examines
the obscure impediments
to what it wants; sees
itself, sees what lies ahead
of itself, and goes forth . . .

RATTLESNAKE

What I remember is a cabin
deep in the woods,
the pure cold air my lungs drank,
and that the earth
was unusually hard, packed tightly
under a thin layer of leaves.

We ate dinner, and I remember
what a child would:
mere flickers, bursts of laughter.
Later, from a window
I heard rustling, harsh words.
You led me to the yard. A snake's head
oozed onto the dirt.
Its blank eyes glinted.
One end and then the other
of the body flexed and whipped
in a twisting rhythm
that dislodged leaves and stones.

When the writhing stopped
you grabbed the snake
and carried it to the kitchen.
After curving a knife along
its quiet belly, you pulled back the skin.
I felt if I looked long enough
I could read what was sprawled there,
tangled and glistening.
Then you tugged the heart
from its nest of arteries and veins
and handed it, still beating, to me.

It was firm and vivid red;
cool, but the pulse sent heat
into my palm. I walked outside
to watch the heart pump
in the eerie sheen of moonlight.

And that's what I have left:
the warm, dull throbbing of a heart
held carefully on my open hand
before I let it fall.

IN THE VALLEY

Let us walk in the valley.
Let us walk with our hands
opened wide in the valley.

Let us gaze at the desert.
Let us not turn to flame
at the eye of the desert.

Let us pass the green mountains
and answer the bones
as they gasp with the wind

Are you last? Are you lone?
Let us hear our own name,
let us find a stone warmed

by the sun in our valley.

AFTER A LINE OF PLATO

I

In the city that shall be perfect,
in the city of intelligence
where thinking reigns

and desire is at rest
and what happens happens
because the self wills it

to be so, you are reading.
I am almost asleep.
The sun slants

on your belly, over your limbs.
I am watching it find circumstance.
I am wondering how fast, how fast,

this abstract energy goes.
Outside, children's shrieks
mix with birdsong and men's saws

and feet back and forth. I am trying
to rise in this cavern of sound
as if with a terrible weight.

The sun swings around
our flesh, armed and glorious,
a procession of ages,

a procession of myth.
If it is true that the clichés follow us
because they have something to say

then this crow on a giant oak tree
makes a very important point.
It croaks a series of harsh notes:

One, two, three.
About our mortality, maybe.
One, two, three.

Or the force of the mind
when it lands on the tree of the body
and believes it owns everything.

One, two, three.
When Satan entered the garden,
he chose a bird

as his initial enchantment, his primary matter,
its black feathers flecked
with iridescence,

all the colors of the garden
playing over its sheen.
He found the highest tree

to peruse his newfound paradise from
and stayed there a very long time
pondering what to begin.

It must have been spring.
The fruits of his provocation
hanging down. The blunt sounds

of animals in the shadows,
fleshly things. A man and a woman
asleep, her dreaming

of difference.
This is the place
where what I am

and what I would like to be
opens its wings . . .
Today is Saturday. The tuliptrees'

pale yellow-greens
bloom unfinished, the fringed palms
of the maple unravel,

tiny, red-veined. Pater says
"the seemingly new is old also"
and "mere matter alone

is nothing." Our crow doesn't know this
as he sends out his song
to a distance that constantly

takes it. He's the detail
unable to see
past its beak. But the devil in us

knows how surely we reside
at the periphery, how foolish
is all speech.

II

And this is what the world is.
Primarily music. Not meaning
but action and form. Not meaning.

In the city of perpetual motion,
in the city that *will* be enough,
the matter itself

has arrived.
It lands in the midst of our innocence.
It lands with its own kind of innocence,

a hard fact beneath it,
the soft air around.
Both the body of stillness

and the body of flight,
poised on a branch
no soul could reach,

with the voice that is not prettiest,
it will sing,
all the colors of the garden

playing over its wings,
while the adequate, more than adequate
promise hangs—

ACKNOWLEDGMENTS

THANKS ARE DUE TO THE EDITORS OF THE FOLLOWING JOURNALS IN WHOSE pages some of these poems appeared: "Rattlesnake" in *Crazyhorse*; "The Growth" and "What the Wind Said to the Girl Who Was Afraid" in *Virginia Quarterly Review*; "Eve, After Eating" and "The Fall" in *Raritan.* Thanks also to editors who published earlier work in the following journals: *Cream City Review, Maryland Poetry Review, Louisiana Literature, Chattahoochee Review, Clockwatch Review.*

I am grateful to the following people, whose encouragement, inspiration, and support have contributed to the making of this book: Larissa Szporluk (the spirit is in the wheels), Neil Arditi, Cynthia Crane, Sydney Blair, John Hollander, William McDonough, Michael Braungart, and my family—especially my mother, Cam Vaughan, a real hammered dulcimer player.

ABOUT THE AUTHOR

LISA WILLIAMS WAS BORN IN NASHVILLE, TENNESSEE IN 1966. AFTER receiving a B.A. degree from Belmont University in 1989, she was awarded an Elliston Fellowship at the University of Cincinnati, where she graduated with an M.A. in Literature in 1992. In 1993, she was awarded a Henry Hoyns Fellowship at the University of Virginia, where she received an M.F.A. in 1996. Other awards for her work include an Academy of American Poets Prize and a Tennessee Williams Scholarship. Her poems have appeared in several literary journals, including *Chattahoochee Review, Louisiana Literature, Raritan,* and *Virginia Quarterly Review.* Currently, Lisa Williams works as a business writer in Charlottesville, Virginia. *The Hammered Dulcimer* is her first book of poems.

THE MAY SWENSON POETRY AWARD WAS NAMED FOR MAY SWENSON, AND honors her as one of America's most provocative, insouciant, and vital poets. During her long career, May published eleven volumes of poems, and she was loved and praised by writers from virtually every major school of poetry. She left a legacy of nearly fifty years of writing when she died in 1989.

May Swenson lived most of her adult life in New York City, the center of poetry writing and publishing in her day. But she is buried in Logan, Utah, her birthplace and hometown.